by Doug Merrilees
& Evelyn Loveday

Technical Consultant
Jack Woolley, Reg. Engr.

Library of Congress Catalog Card Number: 73-89123

International Standard Book Number: 0-88266-020-9

GARDEN WAY PUBLISHING CO., CHARLOTTE, VERMONT 05445

PRINTED IN THE UNITED STATES OF AMERICA

POLE

BUILDING

CONSTRUCTION

ADVANTAGES OF POLE CONSTRUCTION

Many people are becoming interested in pole building construction because they have heard or read that it is relatively cheap and simple. It is, but to understand exactly what it's all about, we should start with a definition:

Pole construction is building in which the vertical, load-bearing members are poles embedded in the ground, and which must be long enough to support the roof. The diameter of the poles usually is about 6 inches at the top ends, and they are spaced much further apart than are the uprights in conventional frame construction. No excavation is necessary beyond digging holes for the poles, and there is no concrete or block foundation. The poles serve the triple function of foundation, bracing and framework, to which the floor (if any), walls and roof all are fastened.

Labor, time and materials all are saved in the pole framing method. Since lateral girts replace the conventional wall studs, and since fewer and longer pieces of lumber are used, the actual framework of the building can be completed quickly. This is a real advantage in bad weather, as the project can be placed under cover rapidly.

Pole buildings have been approved where light frame structures are prohibited because of fire hazard. Pole framing members are so widely separated that fire is unlikely to spread from one to the other. Pole construction is now recognized by all four U.S. model building codes.

Other advantages of pole construction are: It is relatively simple to build and little sawing is necessary. No scaffolding or forms are required during construction, and a minimum of construction labor is needed. In buildings where the loads are relatively light or the spans rather short, lower (hence cheaper) grades of lumber may be used. If the pole holes are dug by hand, only simple hand tools — the kind found in almost any household — are needed.

There are further advantages to this kind of construction in that round timbers have two distinct advantages from the standpoint of strength.

A circular timber is 18 per cent stronger in bending resistance than a rectangular timber of similar grade. A round timber, in practically all cases, possesses a very high proportion of the basic strength of its species. This is because the knots have only half the limiting effect on strength in the natural, round timber form that they do in sawed sections. Tests have shown that full-size round timber poles develop practically the full bending strength of clear wood.

Another advantage of pole frame construction is its high

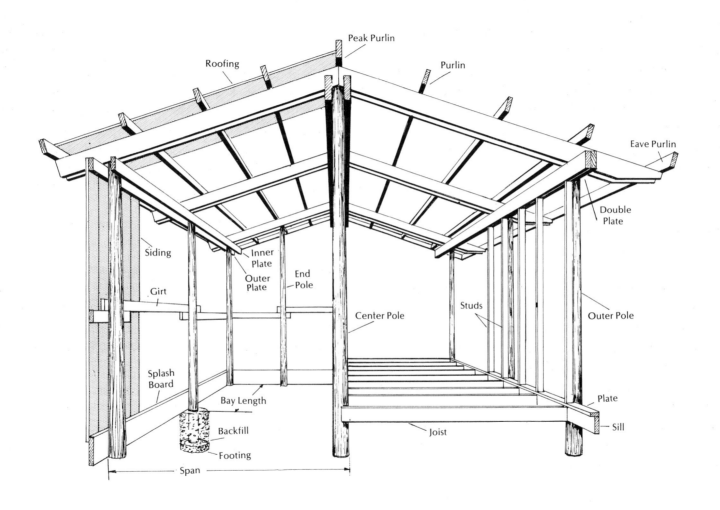

Peak Purlin

Roofing

Purlin

Eave Purlin

Double Plate

Siding

Inner Plate

Outer Plate

End Pole

Girt

Studs

Center Pole

Outer Pole

Splash Board

Bay Length

Plate

Backfill

Joist

Sill

Footing

Span

resistance to wind forces, which results because the poles that support the building are firmly anchored in the ground.

Later in this guide general basic directions are given on how to construct a pole building, and these are followed by some specific plans. Right now it's enough to say that the poles are embedded in the ground, and they must be plumb.

The design of any pole building can be simple enough for unskilled persons to construct. Except for very small buildings, the step of setting the poles, however, is not a project for one person, the reason being that you have only two hands. For this step probably you should hire some unskilled help, which you will supervise, or maybe you can find neighborly help.

In *Vermont Life* Magazine (Summer 1956 issue) there's a story of a pole-type barn-raising after a man's barn burned and his cattle were without shelter. Neighbors helped on the barn (the women cooked), and in two days the poles and main timbers of the new, 80-cow barn were secured, and the majority of the roof was in place.

Once the poles are plumb, the next step is to nail (or bolt) the longitudinal beams to the poles, and make sure the structure is squared up. The roof rafters are connected to this frame, and then your exterior is completed — not forgetting to put on a roof!

What kinds of buildings lend themselves to pole construction? The list is long and includes just about any type of commercial building, such as a warehouse or light manufacturing plant. Then there are farm buildings of all kinds — cow barns, horse barns, cattle sheds, poultry houses, tool sheds and the like. There are homes, too.

Prefabricated pole buildings for commercial and farm use are obtainable from several manufacturers. The purpose of this Guide, however, is to show you how you can do it yourself economically. Later some plans will be pictured in detail, and these will include houses.

It was said earlier that pole construction is relatively simple, but bear in mind the operative word here is "relatively." It would be cheating to give the impression it is as simple as making a sandbox for your youngster. But neither is it nearly as difficult (or expensive) as the conventional type of construction, which requires skilled labor, the use of power tools, and more and costlier materials.

Pole building in varying forms is an age-old type of construction that dates back to the Stone Age, and which has been used in many parts of the world ever since.

Amos Rapoport in *House Form and Culture* says "There are cases where a way of life may lead to . . . a dwelling form related to economic activity rather than climate. For example, the Hidatsa of the Missouri valley were agriculturists from April to November, growing corn, greens and beans. During that period they lived in circular wooden houses 30 to 40 feet in diameter with 5-foot walls made of tree trunks and four central columns 14 feet high supporting rafters carrying branches."

Rapoport goes on to comment on resistance to lateral forces, such as wind or earthquakes, that requires either rigidity or bracing.

"The Fiji islands provide a number of examples of methods of dealing with the lateral force problem. In some

Native Peruvian Pole House

areas the roofs are very simple and supported by central poles as well as peripheral columns. Since these poles are buried deep in the ground, the building acts as a rigid frame, although the flexibility of the members themselves assures some flexibility."

In pole construction the poles actually have an inherent ability to resist wind uplift, especially if the roof framing is very securely attached to them. In areas where hurricanes are expected, the value of this large resistence to uplift that is a part of pole construction should be considered seriously.

Why is there so much current interest in pole construction? There seems to be a batch of good reasons:

1. A limited amount of grading is required, and no excavation beyond digging the pole holes. Thus it can be accomplished without butchering the immediate area, and with a minimum disturbance of the natural surroundings such as tree roots and top soil. Poles also can be driven through fill to firm soil below.

2. Pole construction offers a way to lower building costs by utilizing, if desired, steep hillside locations which present many problems for more conventional construction. There are no delays, either, in waiting for cement foundations to cure, for there are none.

3. As inflation causes the costs of building materials and

labor to climb, there is a very real need for many people to find ways to build more cheaply than before. Pole methods allow such savings.

4. Ever since World War II there has been an ever-increasing interest in self-help. Not only are there many practical advantages to "doing it yourself", but there is a very tangible glow of pride and satisfaction when one completes his own project.

5. With the back-to-the-land movement increasing every year, many people are rejecting expensive and conspicuous life styles. They want and have only the simple tools for living, and are choosing to live in many ways as their ancestors did.

All of this adds up to the reason why pole construction may be the very thing to plan on, whether it is for a home or some other building that you need.

Very little has been published to date on pole construction. In fact it has been said that "the literature is non-existent." This is not quite true, for there are some few publications by wood products associations, which have been consulted here, and which are listed in the references at the back of this Guide.

The modern use of treated poles in the construction of restaurants, churches, schools, recreational cottages and homes began quite recently and as a West Coast phenomenon, gaining impetus with the construction in 1958 of a pole residence in California. Modern methods were learned through the experience of utility and outdoor advertising companies. At the time there was resistance both from lending sources and building code reviewers, but since then enthusiasm for the many advantages of pole construction has mushroomed.

JUST POLES

It's a well known fact that wood deteriorates because of bacteria, insects, fungi and dampness, and to delay such deterioration utility poles and fence posts have long been treated with preservatives. Companies which sell these and poles used in pole buildings strip the bark and then spray them with fungicides, which inhibit the attack of micro-organisms. Then the poles are pressure-impregnated with one of several preservatives.

Such poles can be purchased rather inexpensively, or if you have suitable trees on your own land which can be cut into poles, you can surface-treat them yourself, or better, find a place (inquire at lumber yards) where they can be pressure-treated.

Soft woods are favored for treated poles because they are

porous and accept preservatives better than do the hard woods. Also they are easier to work with in terms of nailing or sawing.

Woods listed as approved for poles to be treated include Western larch, Southern yellow pine, Pacific Coast Douglas fir, lodgepole pine, jack pine, red or Norway pine, ponderosa pine, Western red cedar and Northern white cedar. White pine also is used in the East, as are white and red spruce.

However, if you have a ready access to white or red cedar, locust, redwood heart or cypress, the poles made from these woods will be inherently resistant to rot and micro-organisms. Hemlock also is rot-resistant but is more often used as lumber. These woods need not be pressure-treated, but should have the bark removed.

How long will poles last before deteriorating? This is important, since the poles are the foundation and strength of the structure.

There are varying answers. One firm which manufactures treated poles says: "In the Thirties a well-treated pole was supposed to last 30 years. Now this estimate has risen to 45 to 50 years, since anticipated failures did not occur. The length of service has been achieved under the most severe conditions. Of course, any pole which you use inside your building will be protected, and an even longer life can be expected."

The American Wood Preservers Institute, conducting research for the Department of Housing and Urban Development, prepared the booklet *FHA Pole House Construction*, which sets forth guidelines acceptable to FHA for the construction of pole houses.

The AWPI is a non-profit organization doing research on pressure-treated woods of all kinds for all uses. Their comments on the durability of poles are especially valuable, although their standards are so high that not all manufacturers fully meet them.

AWPI says: "A house erected on poles produced for this purpose, and conforming to the rigid standards described below, is considered permanent — as permanent as a house on a well-constructed concrete foundation. The permanence is achieved by treating the poles with preservative. Using the newly-perfected 'assay method', pole manufacturers now can verify the adequate distribution of preservative in the finished product."

The assay testing method takes borings from the treated poles and subjects them to chemical analysis to determine the amount of preservative present.

AWPI goes on to say that "Users can be assured of the physical and preservative characteristics of the poles if the manufacturer indicates conformance with the AWPI quality control standards by the application of a permanent seal to each pole."

Although all of the preservative treatments have their uses in pole construction, cleanliness, paintability, color and odor will determine the selection for a particular project. The methods are:

Water-borne salt preservatives: They provide clean, odorless, paintable, non-irritating pressure-treated lumber. For poles placed in the ground and subject to leaching, one should be sure to have that treatment which is chemically-bound — not that which is leachable. Recommended by the American Society of Civil Engineers are amoniacal copper arsenite, chromated copper arsenate or chromated zinc arsenate.

Pentachlorophenol in light petroleum solvent: The pole surface is comparatively clean and usually can be painted, provided the wood preserver knows prior to treatment that this is desired. There may be a slight odor until the petroleum has vaporized. This treatment has little effect on the color of the wood.

Pentachlorophenol in volatile petroleum solvent (gasborne treatment): The wood surface also is clean, paintable and odorless, with its color that of the natural wood prior to treatment.

Creosote: The color varies from dark brown to black and the surface often is oily, especially when subjected to higher temperatures. Successful painting is impossible. These factors, plus the creosote odor, make these poles more suitable for use on the exterior of pole buildings. It should be noted that vegetation in direct contact with these poles will be killed for a year or two. Poles so treated are widely used throughout the United States by utility companies and are readily available.

Pentachlorophenol in heavy oil: The pole often has an oily surface, particularly when high temperatures cause an expansion of the liquid petroleum. Pole varies in color from light to dark brown, and an odor usually is present for a period of time. It is often difficult, if not impossible, to paint these poles successfully. Poles treated with this preservative also are readily available, since this too is a common treatment for utility use.

Preservative oils, creosote and the liquid pentachlorophenol petroleum solutions used on poles sometimes travel from the treated wood along nails, and will discolor adjacent plaster or finished flooring. Oil types, however, have a maximum service life.

Tar solutions applied to poles do not penetrate and

preserve the wood. The protection offered, is temporary.

Cuts, such as notches or holes drilled through the preservative zone, should receive several liberal applications of wood preservative to retain the chemical integrity of the pole.

Home builders unable to secure pressure-treated poles can obtain a good degree of protection by soaking in pentachlorophenol solution or creosote (obtainable at hardware or paint stores). A trough may be made of boards, and lined with plastic sheeting. Poles should be dry (not green wood), and the results will be best in hot weather. Wood species naturally rot-resistant may be home-treated also for an added degree of preservation.

HOW TO DO IT

While detailed plans for certain kinds of pole buildings appear in a later section, this may be a good time to run through the steps of pole construction in general. This will give an overview that will help explain what pole construction entails, and what to look for in plans.

This description assumes the building to be on fairly level ground, but with a slight slope for good drainage. It is wise in constructing any building (pole or conventional) to avoid low-lying ground with a high water table. Also avoid heavy, wet clay soil if you can. Sandy gravel is best, as is shown in the tables on pages 11 and 13. Hillside pole construction requires different pole embedment techniques, which are pictured later and are noted by the Tables on page 13.

STARTING

To begin with, of course, all of the tools that will be used, as well as all materials needed for the completed framing and roofing, should be assembled on the site. If you are going to bolt the plates to poles (see Page 17) or pre-bore nail holes (Page 16), a temporary electric power source will be helpful. This is to allow the use of an electric drill and later, in the sheathing work, an electric saw. If the building will not have electric service, of course both functions can be accomplished with hand tools. Hand-boring at elevation for the ridge plates, is difficult, however, when working from a ladder rather than scaffolding.

You start to lay out the building by setting up batter boards at the far corners. Run strings between the batter boards to outline the building.

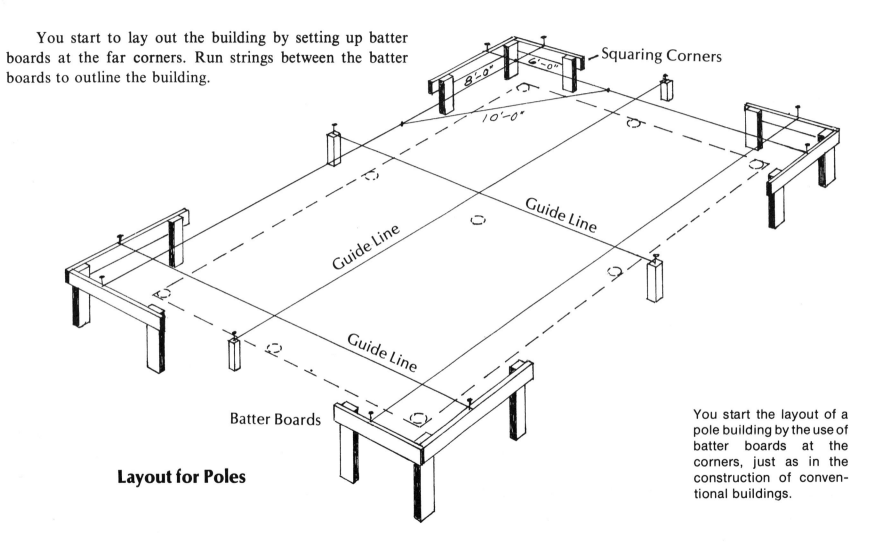

Squaring Corners

8'-0" 6'-0"

10'-0"

Guide Line

Guide Line

Guide Line

Batter Boards

Layout for Poles

You start the layout of a pole building by the use of batter boards at the corners, just as in the construction of conventional buildings.

Square the corners with care by means of a builder's triangle (see illustration) with sides of 6, 8 and 10 feet, or any multiples of 3, 4 and 5 feet. These string guidelines serve to locate the holes for the outer poles.

Determine the location of the poles from the plans, and measure the spacing of poles on the guidelines.

Drop a plumb bob from the measured spacing and, for the outside poles, mark the center of the pole holes 5 or 6 inches **in** from these points by means of small stakes.

When all the pole hole positions are marked by stakes, remove all the interior guidelines. Now you are ready to dig your holes and set the poles. The width of your building will determine whether or not the plans call for interior poles, as well as the type of rafters or trusses needed.

PLANNING THE HOLES

The first thing to consider even before starting to dig, is the general soil condition of the site; secondly its grade.

In general for any pole building, the soil is considered below average if it is soft clay, poorly compacted sand, or clay containing large amounts of silt (with water standing during a wet period). Average soil is compact, well-graded sand and gravel, hard clay or graded fine and coarse sand.

Pole buildings based on the criteria in Table A are suitable on sites that are flat or with a grade of less than 1 in 10. In all the Tables:

H=Unsupported height of poles (from ground to first cross member).

A=Embedment depth, using backfill or tamped earth, sand, gravel or crushed rock.

B=Embedment depth, using backfill of concrete or soil cement.

D=Bearing Diameter (size of pad).

TABLE A

"H"	Pole Spacing	Good Soil				Average Soil				Below Average Soil			
		Embedment Depth		"D"	Tip Size	Embedment Depth		"D"	Tip Size	Embedment Depth		"D"	Tip Size
		A	B			A	B			A	B		
1-1/2'	8'	5.0'	4.0'	18"	6.5"	6"	5.0'	24"	6"	---	6.0'	36"	6"
to	10'	5.5'	4.0'	21"	7"	7.0'	5.0'	30"	7"	---	6.5'	42"	7"
3'	12'	6.0'	4.5'	24"	7"	7.5'	5.5'	36"	7"	---	7.0'	48"	7"
3'	8'	6.0'	4.0'	18"	7"	7.5'	5.5'	24"	7"	---	7.0'	36"	7"
to	10'	6.0'	4.5'	21"	8"	8.0'	6.0'	30"	8"	---	7.5'	42"	8"
8'	12'	6.5'	5.0'	24"	8"	---	6.0'	36"	8"	---	8.0'	48"	8"

--- Embedment depth required is greater than 8 feet, and considered excessively expensive.

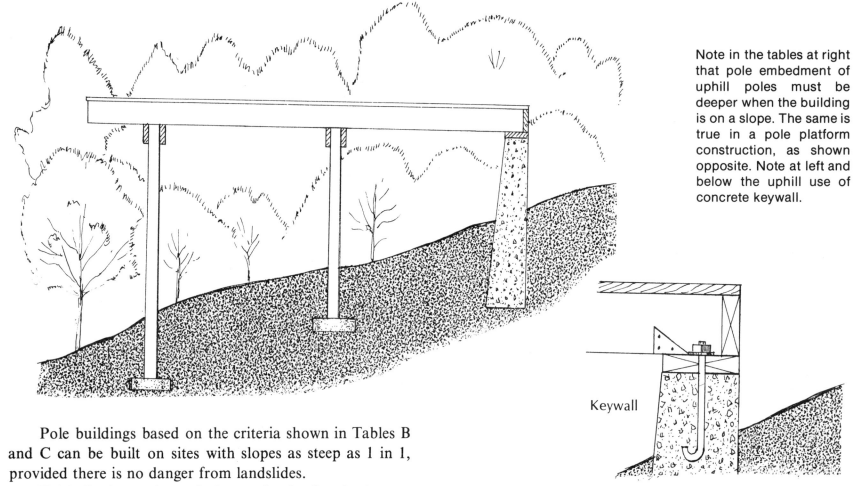

Note in the tables at right that pole embedment of uphill poles must be deeper when the building is on a slope. The same is true in a pole platform construction, as shown opposite. Note at left and below the uphill use of concrete keywall.

Keywall

Pole buildings based on the criteria shown in Tables B and C can be built on sites with slopes as steep as 1 in 1, provided there is no danger from landslides.

Table B shows the embedment depths for the longer, downhill poles, which carry only vertical loads.

TABLE B

Soil Strength	Slope of Grade		
	Up to 1:3	Up to 1:2	Up to 1:1
Below Average	4.5'	6.0'	---
Average	4.0'	5.0'	7.0'
Good	4.0'	4.0'	6.0'

Table C shows the criteria for the uphill line of poles in a steep site, that must be embedded adequately to resist lateral as well as vertical loads.

TABLE C

"H"	Pole Spacing	Good Soil				Average Soil				Below Average Soil			
		Embedment Depth		"D"	Tip Size	Embedment Depth		"D"	Tip Size	Embedment Depth		"D"	Tip Size
		A	B			A	B			A	B		
1-1/2' to 3'	6'	7.0'	5.0'	18"	8"	---	6.5'	18"	8"	---	---	--	--
	8'	7.5'	5.5'	18"	9"	---	7.0'	24"	9"	---	---	--	--
	10'	---	6.0'	21"	9"	---	8.0'	30"	9"	---	---	--	--
	12'	---	6.5'	24"	10"*	---	---	--	--	---	---	--	--
3' to 8'	6'	7.5'	5.5'	18"	8"	---	7.0'	18"	8"	---	---	--	--
	8'	8.0'	6.0'	18"	9"	---	8.0'	24"	9"	---	---	--	--
	10'	---	7.0'	21"	10"*	---	---	--	--	---	---	--	--
	12'	---	7.0'	24"	11"*	---	---	--	--	---	---	--	--

— Embedment depth required is greater than 8 feet, and considered excessively expensive.

* These tip diameters may be decreased by one inch providing embedment is increased by one-half foot.

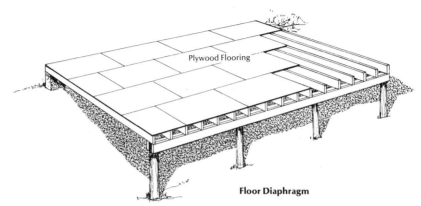

Plywood Flooring

Floor Diaphragm

Pole platforms (those on which conventional frame buildings rest) are based on the criteria shown in Table D. They are suitable on sites with a flat grade, or less than a 1 in 10 slope.

TABLE D

"H"	Pole Spacing	Good Soil				Average Soil			Below Average Soil			
		Embedment Depth		"D"	Tip Size	Embedment Depth		"D"	Tip Size	Embedment Depth		"D"	Tip Size
		A	B			A	B			A	B		
1-1/2' to 3'	8'	4.0'	4.0'	18"	5"	5.5'	4.0'	24"	5"	7.0'	5.0'	36"	5"
	10'	4.5'	4.0'	21"	5"	6.0'	4.0'	30"	5"	8.0'	5.5'	42"	5"
	12'	5.0'	4.0'	24"	5"	6.5'	4.5'	36"	5"	---	5.5'	48"	5"
3' to 8'	8'	5.0'	4.0'	18"	6"	6.5'	4.5'	24"	6"	---	6.0'	36"	6"
	10'	5.5'	4.0'	21"	7"	7.0'	5.0'	30"	7"	---	6.5'	42"	7"
	12'	6.0'	4.5'	24"	7"	7.5'	5.5'	36"	7"	---	7.0'	48"	7"

— Embedment depth required is greater than 8 feet, and considered excessively expensive.

DIGGING THE POLE HOLES

Digging pole holes may be done by hand or by one of several mechanical means. Hand digging or very careful machine digging protects tree roots, top soil and the soil structure around the poles.

Poles taper, and you will set the larger or butt ends in the ground. Dig holes 6 to 8 inches larger in diameter than the butt of the pole. If the holes are of any considerable depth, however, they will have to be wider than that to allow digging room, unless a power auger or pole shovels are used.

A general rule of thumb is that the depth of the pole in the ground should be 4 feet when the eaves of the building will not be over 10 feet from the ground. When the eaves will be more than 10 feet, the poles should be embedded to a depth of 5 feet. However, the most important guide to the depth of the poles is the frost line in your locality. In Vermont, for instance, poles for any building should be embedded at least 4 feet, regardless of where the eaves are. Also, as shown in Tables B and C (page 13), poles for hillside buildings require deeper embedment than those for a level site.

In selecting your poles you will find those of 5 or 6 inches in diameter at the top are adequate for most buildings. For any pole up to 16 feet in length, a 4 or 5-inch top diameter will be sufficient. The pole always should be 2 or 3 feet longer than the distance from the bottom of the hole to the roof. The top later will be cut off flush with the rafters.

SETTING THE POLES

Your plan or the soil condition may require that in each pole hole you have a concrete pad at the bottom. A good rule here is to pour the pad half as thick as the diameter of the hole. Do not set the poles until the concrete has cured.

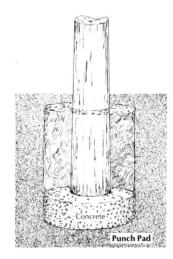

Heavy flat stone or poured cement punch pad should be provided for each of the pole holes before the poles are placed.

Pick out the straightest poles for the corners of the building. Then with block and tackle (and/or a few strong friends) insert the outside poles first. Then insert the inside poles if they are required.

Rotate each pole so that the straightest side faces out. Use a wrapped rope and wood lever bar. A peavey may tear the wood. Shovel a small amount of soil around the pole and tamp lightly — just enough to keep the butt end from shifting. Complete embedment of the poles is not done at this time.

Align the poles vertically with a carpenter's level placed on a straight-edge held against the outer face. Nail temporary braces to the poles and to stakes in the ground, to keep the poles lined up until framing is completed. Locate this bracing in areas where it won't interfere with the work.

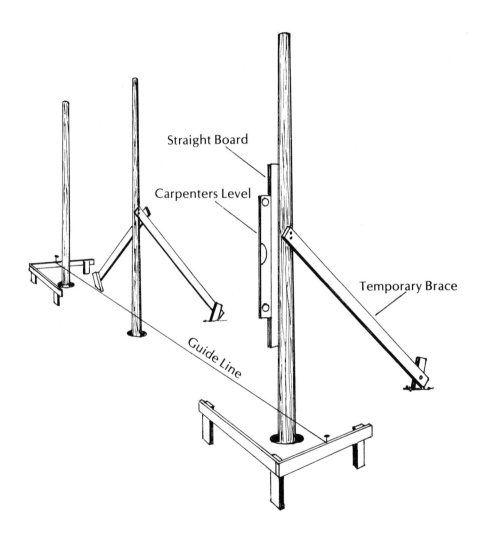

Straight Board

Carpenters Level

Temporary Brace

Guide Line

Alignment of the poles is a very important step and must be done correctly. Normally the *outside* edge of the poles — those facing away from the building — must be vertical. However, if the building is to be sheathed inside (see discussion on Page 34), the *inside* pole edges must be vertical.

WALL PLATES

The outside plates at the eaves should be attached first. Determine the height for these plates by measuring up from a level line this way:

Drive a nail in a pole a few inches above the highest point of ground. With a straight-edge and carpenter's level establish this level point on all the poles in the wall. Nail a 2 x 4 or a 2 x 6 cleat (about 36 inches long) with its top flush with the measured height from your ground line to the bottom of the plate's intended location. This cleat is temporary.

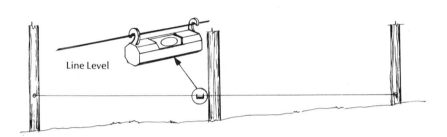

At left and above are shown two methods of establishing the ground level and location of eave plates.

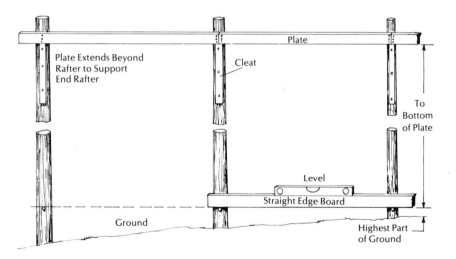

Plates should be cut so that their ends will butt together at the poles, with the exception of the plates at the corners. These should be extended beyond the poles on the long sides of the building to support the end rafters on the outsides of the poles.

Rest the plates on the cleats and nail or bolt them to the poles. Now remove the temporary cleats. Pre-boring the nail holes in the plates will minimize the danger of splitting the wood, yet will not decrease the holding power. Use a 5/32-inch drill for 40-d nails. Plates on the inside of the wall poles are not attached until the rafters are in place.

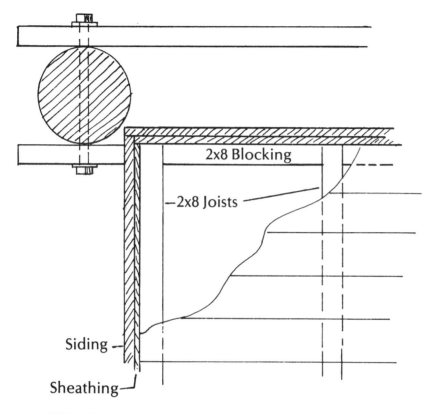

2x8 Blocking

—2x8 Joists

Siding

Sheathing

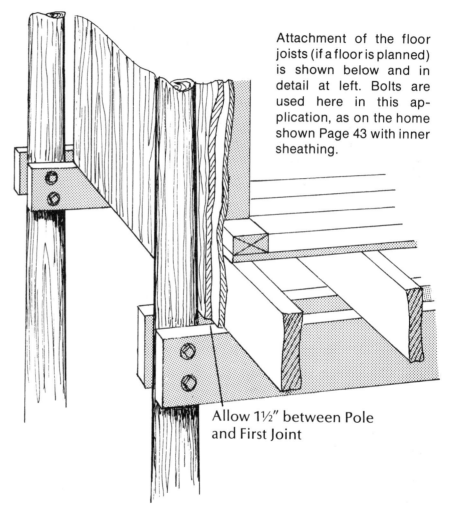

Attachment of the floor joists (if a floor is planned) is shown below and in detail at left. Bolts are used here in this application, as on the home shown Page 43 with inner sheathing.

Allow 1½" between Pole and First Joint

When heavy snow weight or exceptional winds may be expected, or where load-bearing floors are supported by the poles, bolts are advised instead of nailing to attach plates and floor sills to the poles. Lag screws with washers may be so used, also.

RIDGE PLATES

Follow the same general procedure for the ridge plates as you did for the wall plates. Determine the height of the bottom of the ridge plates (as for the wall plates), and nail cleats of 2x4 lumber on each side of the center pole. Rest the plates on the cleats and proceed to fasten them as with the wall plates with spikes, bolts or lag screws.

If the building has center poles, locate ridge plates first on the outside poles. Then a taut string run between them, as shown at the right, will easily establish the location for the ridge plates on the center poles.

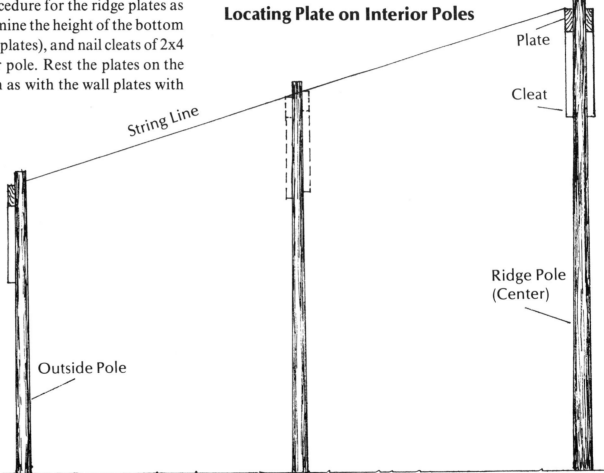

Locating Plate on Interior Poles

Plate

String Line

Cleat

Ridge Pole (Center)

Outside Pole

INNER POLE PLATES

When the building is so wide as to require extra inner poles, the position of the plates on these intermediate poles should be located by running a line from the ridge plate to the wall plate. Attach cleats and plates on both sides to correspond with this line.

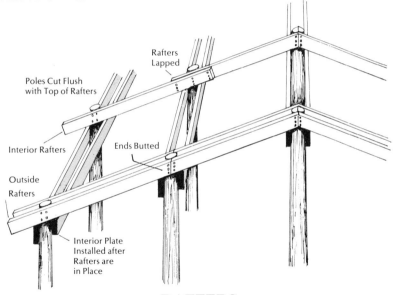

Poles Cut Flush with Top of Rafters

Rafters Lapped

Interior Rafters

Ends Butted

Outside Rafters

Interior Plate Installed after Rafters are in Place

RAFTERS

Rafters are placed on the outside of the end wall poles and should be butted to provide a smooth base for exterior siding.

Attachment of rafters above the pole plates is shown at left, and in detail below, rafter overhang at eaves.

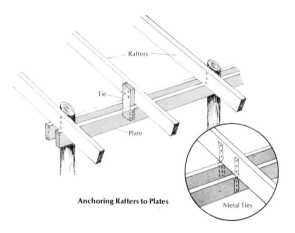

Rafters

Tie

Plate

Anchoring Rafters to Plates

Metal Ties

Extend the lower rafters over the outside plates at the eaves to provide an overhang — usually about 10 to 14 inches. Cut the butt ends of the outside rafters to the proper angle so that the rafters may be nailed to the poles. Intermediate rafters may be lapped. Rafters adjacent to a pole should be nailed to the pole.

When rafters are in place, the poles should be cut off flush with the tops of the rafters. Anchor other rafters to the plates by means of metal straps or by 2-inch scab boards (or ties), fitted between the rafters.

POLE EMBEDMENT

Proper setting and embedment of the poles is crucial to the strength of the building's frame. After the rafters are in place, now complete the pole embedment.

You may backfill around the poles with the soil dug from the holes, or the backfilling may be done with concrete, soil cement, pea gravel or crushed rock. Clean sand is least expensive and achieves 100 per cent compaction when flooded with water, providing the surrounding soil offers good drainage.

When earth is used it must be compacted, a little at a time, by wetting and careful tamping. Over-embedding, however, or use of too much concrete, defeats the inherent economy of the pole system.

Backfilling with soil cement is an economical way of achieving strength nearly equal to concrete. It is made by using earth free of organic matter and sifted to remove all pieces over one inch in size. Mix five parts of earth with one of cement. Then wet and mix it to a thick slurry and tamp it well into place around the poles.

Another method of embedment uses a "necklace" of concrete around the pole below the frost line. It can be cast after the poles are set but not fully filled in. This necklace should be at least 12 inches thick. A minimum of four one-inch diameter lag screws around the pole are required to transfer the vertical force to the necklace.

The necklace method is practical only in areas where the frost line does not exceed 2 feet. It would be exceedingly difficult to cast such a necklace at a depth of three feet or more.

When embedment of the poles has been completed the temporary pole braces are removed.

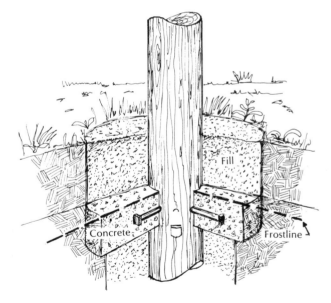

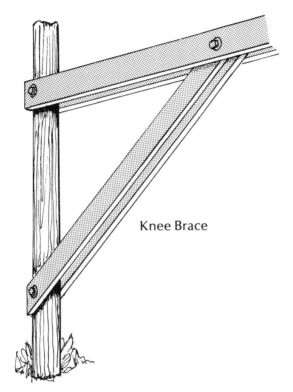

Knee Brace

INSIDE WALL PLATES

After the lower rafters are in place, the inside plates on the eaves should be installed. Push the plates up against the rafters and nail them to the poles, as shown in the illustration for rafters.

PERMANENT BRACING

Knee braces or plywood gussets should be installed on the inside poles. Nail two pieces of 2 x 4 four feet long at each end, as illustrated. When there is a wide center space in the structure an additional knee brace or gusset should be attached to the

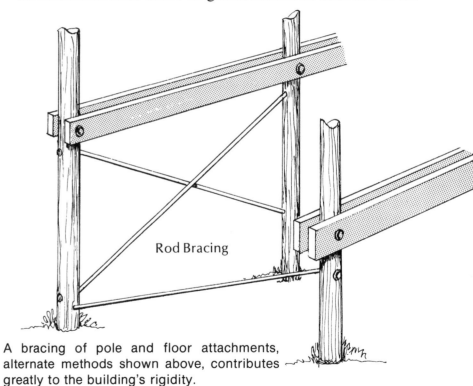

Rod Bracing

A bracing of pole and floor attachments, alternate methods shown above, contributes greatly to the building's rigidity.

pole on each side of the center space, as shown. Gussets are better than knee bracing, since they provide greater strength at the hinge points, and they are no more difficult to cut and install.

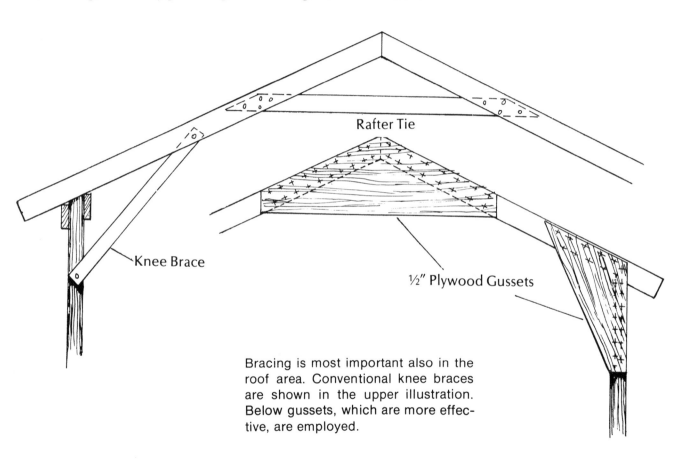

Rafter Tie

Knee Brace

½" Plywood Gussets

Bracing is most important also in the roof area. Conventional knee braces are shown in the upper illustration. Below gussets, which are more effective, are employed.

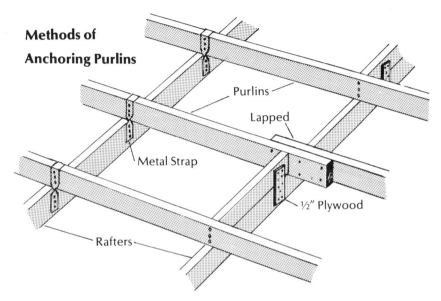

Methods of Anchoring Purlins

Purlins

Lapped

Metal Strap

½" Plywood

Rafters

ROOF SHEATHING

When rafters are spaced 2 feet on center (2 feet apart), no purlins are needed and 1-inch sheathing of ½-inch plywood of sheathing grade may be used.

When rafters are spaced further apart, purlins are needed for 1-inch wood sheathing, metal or other types of roofing. Purlins are laid across the rafters and either are lapped or butted, as shown. Rafters or purlins may be spaced up to 8 feet apart when 2-inch roof decking is used.

SIDE WALL CONSTRUCTION

If you want to have your pole building fully enclosed to the ground, start at the ground with splash boards. This is true whether you are planning an enclosed farm building, or to put skirting around the poles on which a house is built.

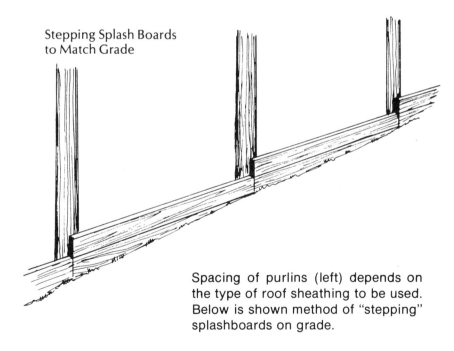

Stepping Splash Boards to Match Grade

Spacing of purlins (left) depends on the type of roof sheathing to be used. Below is shown method of "stepping" splashboards on grade.

Starting about 3 inches under the ground line and extending up the wall, spike splash boards to the poles, using pressure-treated lumber or wood that is inherently rot-resistant (see page 7). These should be one or two 2 x 10 or 2 x 12 planks.

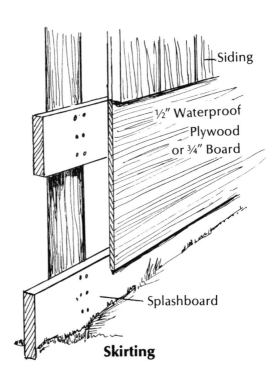

Skirting

Detail of splashboards and of exterior sheathing method is shown at the left. Note pressure - treated lumber should be placed below the ground line. In areas where there are termites use asbestos cement board buried in the earth. To the right is illustrated the use of girts between the poles to support the sidewall sheathing. Shown in cross-section is the reinforcement of a girt.

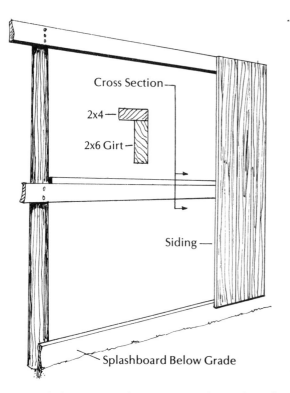

Girts for the siding are nailed across the poles above the splash boards. They should be spaced on 2 feet or 4 feet, depending upon the type of siding to be used. Generally speaking, metal siding will require 2-foot centers, while wood can be on 4-foot centers.

If the space between poles exceeds 6 feet a 2 x 4 is placed (as illustrated) on each 2 x 6 for reinforcement. However, metal siding always will require more reinforcing than wood.

Vertical boards and battens (or other kinds of siding such as plywood or metal) then are attached to the girts. In any case, the top two inches of the splash boards should be overlapped by the side walls.

Year-'round home is likely to have a utility room base.

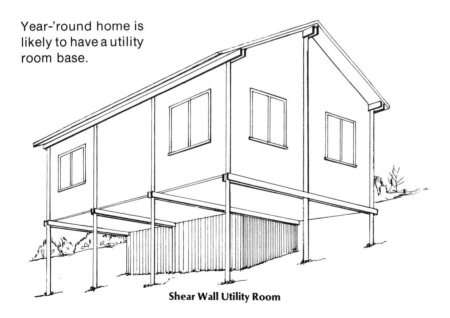

Shear Wall Utility Room

FLOOR CONSTRUCTION AND INSULATION

Most pole buildings, unless a dirt floor is in order, will have a slab floor (see bottom illustration on Page 27) or a suspended floor, and if these buildings are to be located and used in cold climate areas, construction should be planned with the view to effective floor insulation. Methods of suspended floor joist attachment are shown on Page 26, while those which are illustrated on Page 17 will provide for greater floor loading. The chart on Page 28 provides safe formulae of load and support for both floors and roofs. In cold country take into account the weight of possible snow accumulations, particularly if the roof pitch is shallow.

In slab floor construction do not overlook the need to lay a vapor barrier of polyethylene sheeting under the slab. Otherwise the slab will absorb ground moisture, and some serious problems may develop later.

In climates where termites occur, ring cups may be placed around the poles and the wall skirting is not run down to the ground level.

FRAMING FOR FLOORS

Floors carrying heavy loads (see chart Page 28) will be stronger if supported by bolt or lag screw attachment, as shown on Page 17. The butting of joists to the sill plates, attached with metal strapping as shown at the left below, would not be used except where light floor loads are planned. The overlapped joists shown at right below rest on and are supported by the sill plates, and will have a greater load capacity.

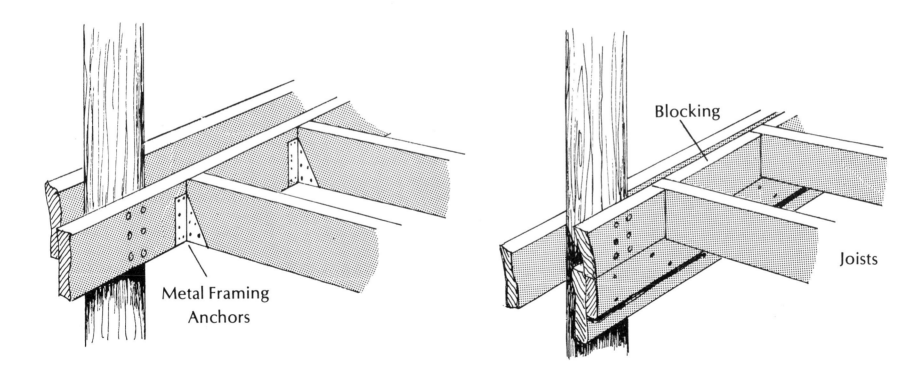

Metal Framing Anchors

Blocking

Joists

FLOOR INSULATION

Methods of insulating suspended floors and those of slab construction are indicated below. See details on the latter also on **Page 25**. Note at left the use of dead air space to supplement the insulation.

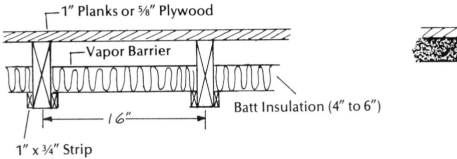

1" Planks or ⅝" Plywood
Vapor Barrier
Batt Insulation (4" to 6")
16"
1" x ¾" Strip

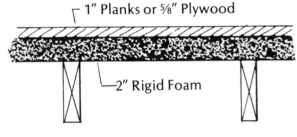

1" Planks or ⅝" Plywood
2" Rigid Foam

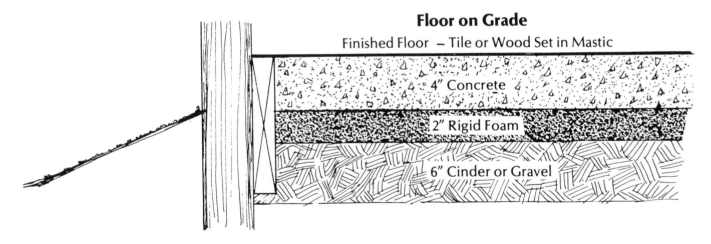

Floor on Grade

Finished Floor — Tile or Wood Set in Mastic
4" Concrete
2" Rigid Foam
6" Cinder or Gravel

MAXIMUM SPAN FLOOR JOISTS & RAFTERS
SPACED 16 " ON CENTERS

Timber Size	Span in Feet Eastern Spruce	Span in Feet Douglas Fir	Timber Size	Span in Feet Eastern Spruce	Span in Feet Douglas Fir
2 x 6	8	10	2 x 6	10	11
2 x 8n	10	12	3 x 8	13	14
2 x 10	13	15	3 x 10	16	18
2 x 12	16	18	3 x 12	20	22
2 x 14	19	21	3 x 15	22	24

NOTE: Two planks spiked together doubles the strength factor.
Adding a center support more than doubles the strength.

ROOF INSULATION

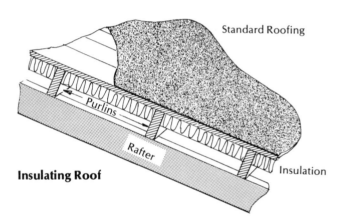

Insulating Roof

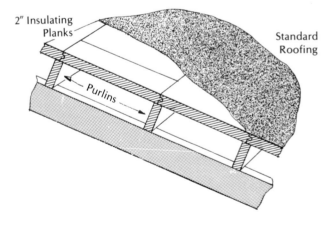

This, then, is the general summary of pole construction, and the methods are the same whether you're building a chicken coop or a house.

Garden Way Associates' industrial designer, who illustrated the preceeding pages, has prepared plans of example pole buildings, which follow.

Other plans may be obtained from some of the sources listed under *References*, or, now that you have the basics in mind, you can design your own pole building.

REFERENCES

American Wood Preservers Institute, *Pole House Construction,* McLean, Va. Undated.

Anderson, L. O. & Harold F. Zornig, *Build Your Own Low-Cost Home.* Dover Publications, Inc., New York, 1972.

Cornell University, Ithaca, N.Y., Bulletin No. 401, *Pole Barn Construction.* Undated.

Kern, Ken, *The Owner-Built Home.* Oakhurst, California. 1972

Lees, Al, The Lockbox House. Popular Science Magazine, May, July, September, November, 1972.

Oregon State University Cooperative Extension Service, *Pole Type Structures.* 1968.

Patterson, Donald, *Pole Building Design.* American Wood Preservers Inst., McLean, Va. 1969.

Rapoport, Amos, *House Form and Culture.* Prentice Hall, Ins. Englewood Cliffs, N.J. 1969.

Roberts, Rex, *Your Engineered House.* M. Evans & Co., New York. 1964.

Southern Forest Products Ass'n., *How to Build Pole Type Frame Buildings.* New Orleans, La. Undated.

Norum, W.A., *Pole Buildings Go Modern.* Proceedings of the American Society of Civil Engineers, Journal of the Structural Division, April 1967.

POLE BUILDING PLANS

Storage Shed I
Vacation Cottage II
Year 'Round Home III

I

PLANS

STORAGE SHED

This shed is designed to give you some practical experience in basic pole building as well as providing additional storage space. No attempt has been made to design this for a specific need, but it could be adapted or fitted out for use as a barn for animals or as a tool shop. Refer to government bulletins or the many books published on specific needs of goats, chickens, etc.

The poles need not be larger than 7 inches at the base for this small building, but all other directions and suggestions in the preceding text should be followed. The best roofing for this type of building considering the shallow slope is "double-coverage" roll roofing. Roughly half of each three foot strip is smooth tar-coated and the balance has a crushed mineral surface. Start at the lower side of the roof with the smooth portion of a length of the roll. (The coated half will be used to finish at the peak of the roof.) Cement this down with quick setting asphalt cement, trimming to the roof edges. A full strip is now laid over this and nailed at the top edge in two 8 inch rows with nails 12 inches apart. Trim at edges, leaving 1/4 to 3/8 inch overhang. Continue on to the peak of the roof, finishing with the balance of the first strip.

The siding can be any of several textured plywoods, such as texture 1-11, or tongue and groove siding, or the board and batten type. Windows are difficult to build, and it will be easier to buy some from a salvage building material yard or one of the various stock sizes from a lumber yard.

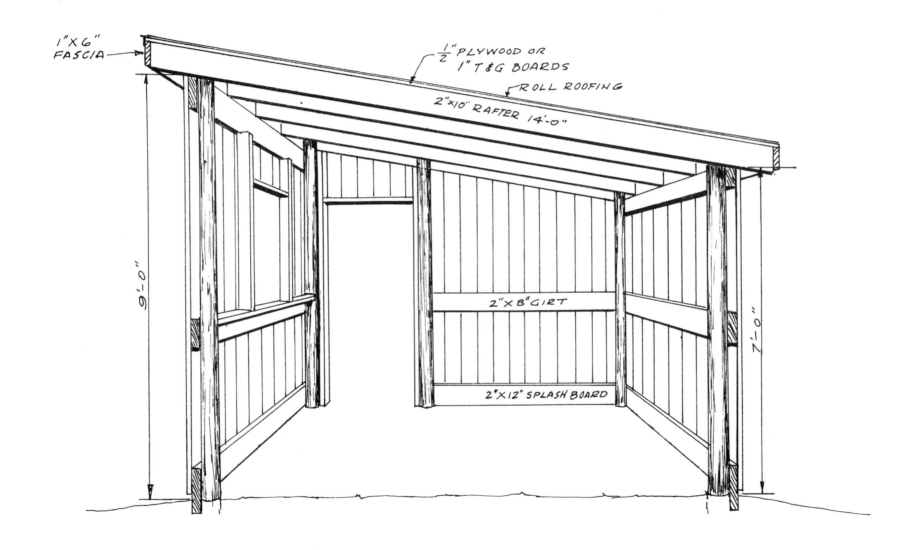

1"X 6"
FASCIA

½" PLYWOOD OR
1" T & G BOARDS

ROLL ROOFING

2"X10" RAFTER 14'-0"

2"X 8" GIRT

2"X 12" SPLASH BOARD

9'-0"

7'-0"

33

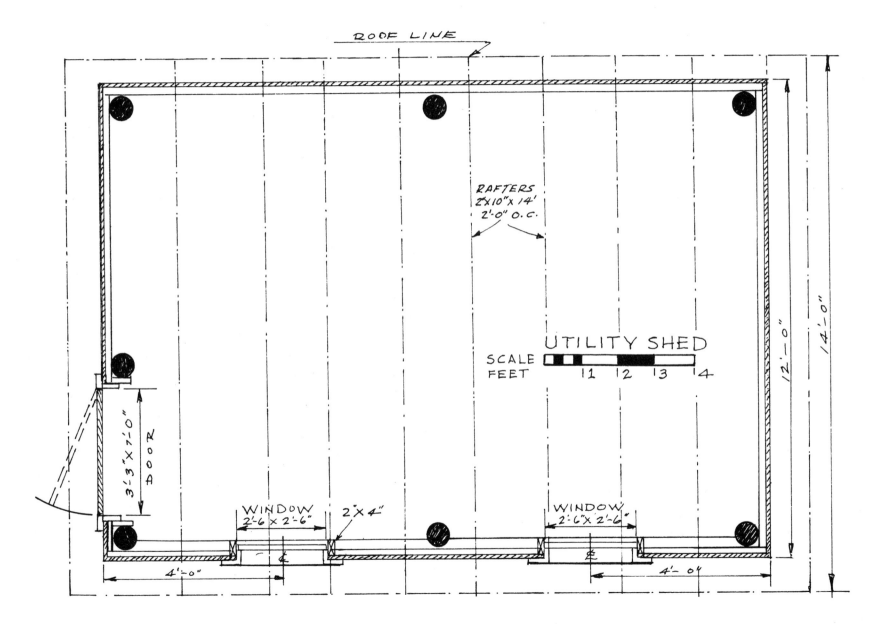

ROOF LINE

RAFTERS
2"X10"X 14'
2'-0" O.C.

UTILITY SHED
SCALE
FEET |1 |2 |3 |4

12'-0"

14'-0"

3'-3"X7'-0" DOOR

WINDOW
2'-6" X 2'-6"

2"X 4"

WINDOW
2'-6" X 2'-6"

4'-0"

4'-0"

II

PLANS

VACATION COTTAGE

This cottage has been laid out to take advantage of standard construction lumber, which comes in increments of two feet. If you want to change the outside dimensions, keep this in mind, to avoid needless waste.

One modification of previous text instructions is very important: Because of the natural taper of poles, it is difficult to enclose them in walls. So in this and the following design the poles are left *outside* the building proper. The poles must be set vertical to the *inside* face rather than the outside as shown on Page 15 and 16.

One of the advantages of a pole building is that none of the walls is load-bearing, so that the partitions and even outside walls can be changed at will without affecting the basic structure. The sequence of building would be: poles erected, plates attached at eaves and floor levels, followed by joists, rafters, roofing and flooring. At this stage you have a solid platform sheltered by a roof. Walls and partitions now can be constructed on this platform out of the elements.

Modifications to be considered might include eliminating the clerestory windows by raising or dropping the peak at the center line of the building, though this would diminish its attractiveness, and also the ventilation and light which such clerestory windows provide.

All studding (2 x 4's) is two feet on centers to take advantage of the standard four-foot width of most plywood and panelling.

(Continued on Page 38)

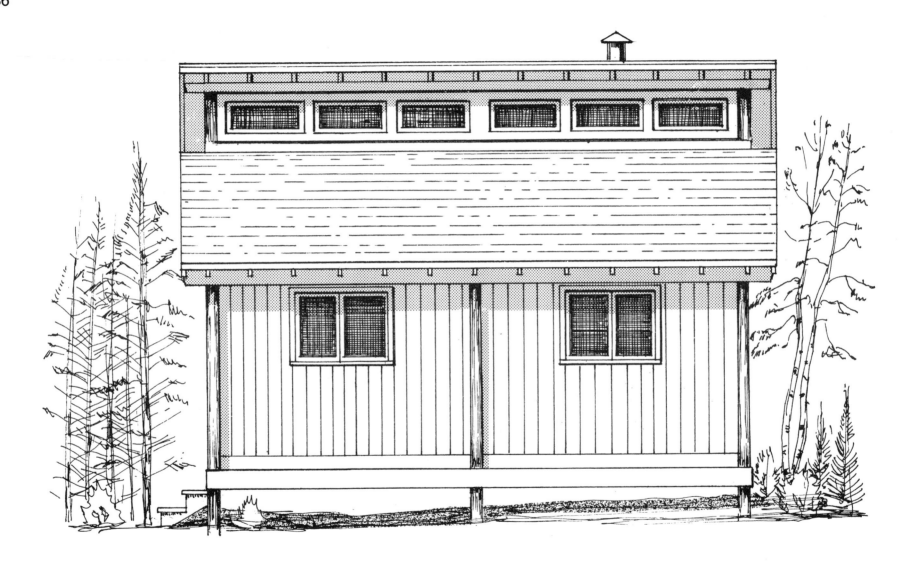

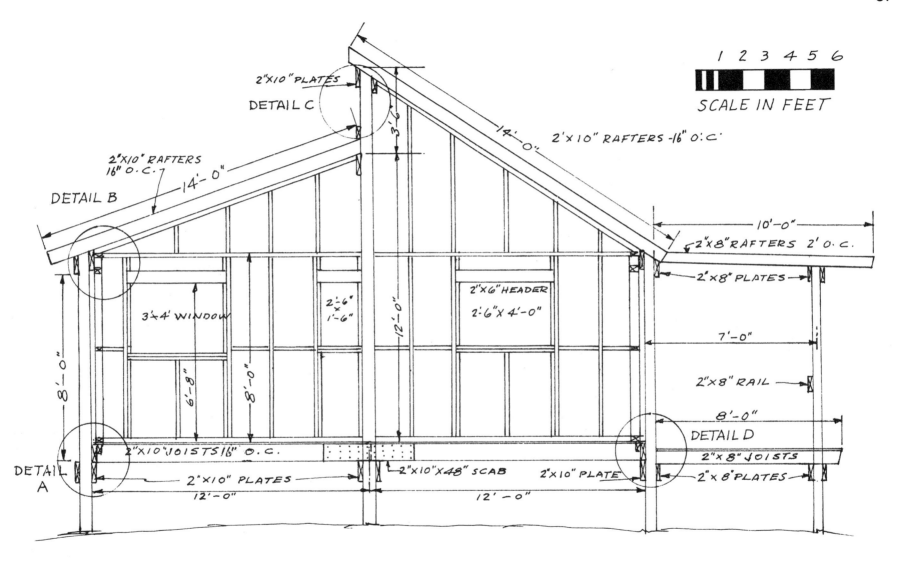

2"x10" PLATES

DETAIL C

1 2 3 4 5 6

SCALE IN FEET

2'x10" RAFTERS -16" O.C.

2"x10" RAFTERS 16" O.C.

DETAIL B

14'-0"

14'-0"

3'-6"

10'-0"

2"x8" RAFTERS 2'0.C.

2"x8" PLATES

3'x4' WINDOW

2'-6" x 1'-6"

2"x6" HEADER
2'-6" x 4'-0"

12'-0"

7'-0"

2"x8" RAIL

6'-8"

8'-0"

8'-0"

8'-0"

DETAIL D

8'-0"

2"x10" JOISTS 16" O.C.

2"x8" JOISTS

DETAIL A

2"x10" PLATES

2"x10"x48" SCAB

2"x10" PLATE

2"x8" PLATES

12'-0"

12'-0"

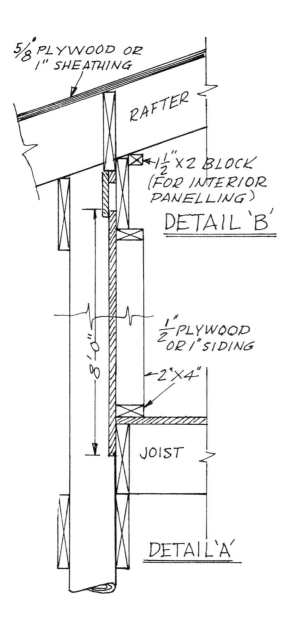

⁵⁄₈" PLYWOOD OR 1" SHEATHING

RAFTER

1½" X 2 BLOCK (FOR INTERIOR PANELLING)

DETAIL 'B'

½" PLYWOOD OR 1" SIDING

2" X 4"

8'-0"

JOIST

DETAIL 'A'

(Continued From Page 34)

Window sizes are suggested only, and accurate rough opening sizes should be checked when ordering windows.

Any of various siding materials can be used, and insulation and inside finish can be added at your convenience. Refer to drawings P. 25, 27 & 28.

Like the Year 'Round Home (plans to follow) this Vacation Cottage is sheathed on the insides of the poles. This is so that interior insulation and wall finish may be added if desired. This might be particularly useful in cold areas should the owner wish to use the cottage in the late fall or the winter. The major problem encountered then would be the protection of water and drainage lines.

If such a conversion is a real possibility, the builder might well modify these plans to the extent of including a below-frost line utility base, through which such water and drain lines are passed. This also would provide a solid and ready-made base for furnace and/or fireplace, should they be wanted later. Well tiles sunk below frost and brought up to floor level, if well-insulated also will provide adequate pipe protection.

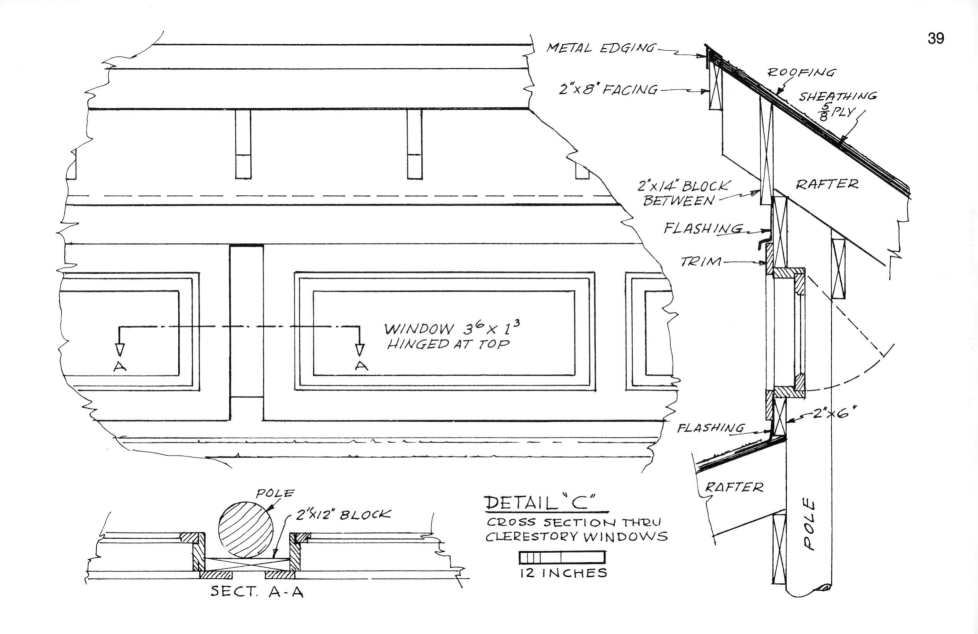

METAL EDGING

ROOFING

2"x8" FACING

SHEATHING
5/8 PLY

2"x14" BLOCK
BETWEEN

RAFTER

FLASHING

TRIM

WINDOW 3⁶ x 1³
HINGED AT TOP

$3^6 \times 1^3$

FLASHING

2"x6"

RAFTER

POLE

POLE

2"x12" BLOCK

SECT. A-A

DETAIL "C"
CROSS SECTION THRU
CLERESTORY WINDOWS

12 INCHES

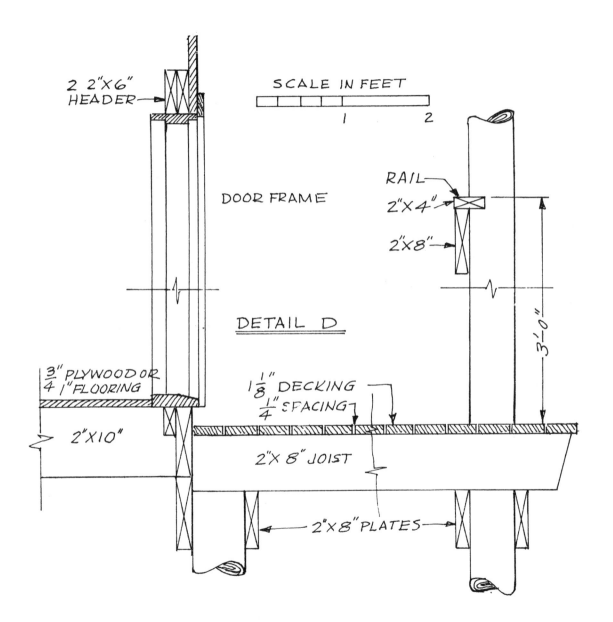

2 2"X6"
HEADER

SCALE IN FEET

1   2

DOOR FRAME

RAIL
2"X4"

2"X8"

DETAIL D

3'-0"

$\frac{3}{4}$" PLYWOOD OR
$1\frac{1}{4}$" FLOORING

$1\frac{1}{8}$" DECKING
$\frac{1}{4}$" SPACING

2"X10"

2"X 8" JOIST

2"X8" PLATES

When building exterior porches or decks — such as on the Year 'Round Home, next — the use of naturally resistant woods (see Page 7) or even better the use of pressure - treated lumber for both the deck boards and floor joists will avoid much maintenance and later grief.

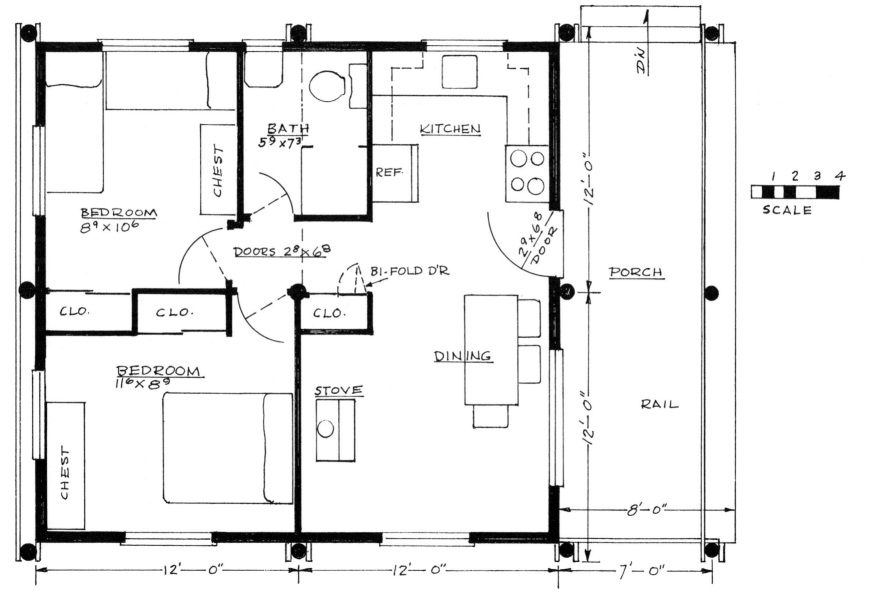

BEDROOM
$8^9 \times 10^6$

BATH
$5^9 \times 7^3$

KITCHEN

CHEST

REF.

DOORS $2^8 \times 6^8$

$2^9 \times 6^8$ DOOR

BI-FOLD D'R

CLO.

CLO.

CLO.

DN

PORCH

12'-0"

BEDROOM
$11^6 \times 8^9$

STOVE

DINING

CHEST

RAIL

12'-0"

8'-0"

12'- 0"

12'- 0"

7'- 0"

1 2 3 4

SCALE

III
PLANS

YEAR 'ROUND HOME

Locating a pole building on a suitable slope provides a dividend of a carport and a storage area, as shown in these drawings. This house uses roof trusses to achieve a spaciousness unusual for a relatively small house. Many lumber yards build standard trusses which, if purchased, would save a great deal of time and labor. If you want to do this part yourself, make a master pattern and follow it closely, so that each truss will be the same. It is important to use plenty of nails and to coat every joint with a resorcinol glue. Glue itself has become much more widely used in home construction, the flooring and wall panelling in particular being secured with glue as well as nails.

As with the Vacation Cottage, all walls and partitions are non load-bearing, and the plans can be modified easily to suit a family's needs. A major difference is the ground floor storage and furnace room, through which all water and drainage lines must run. Bathroom and kitchen must be located above this room, and in colder climates a concrete foundation below the frost line would be advisable.

Changing the roof structure to standard pole construction involves long enough center poles to form the peak, and adding the peak plates. Rafters should be 2 x 10's sixteen inches on centers. Refer to Drawings on Pages 27 and 28 for floor and roof insulation. Our advising engineer recommends 12 inches of insulation for floors in the North and 6 inches between the trusses.

SIDE ELEVATION

1 2 3 4 5
SCALE IN FEET

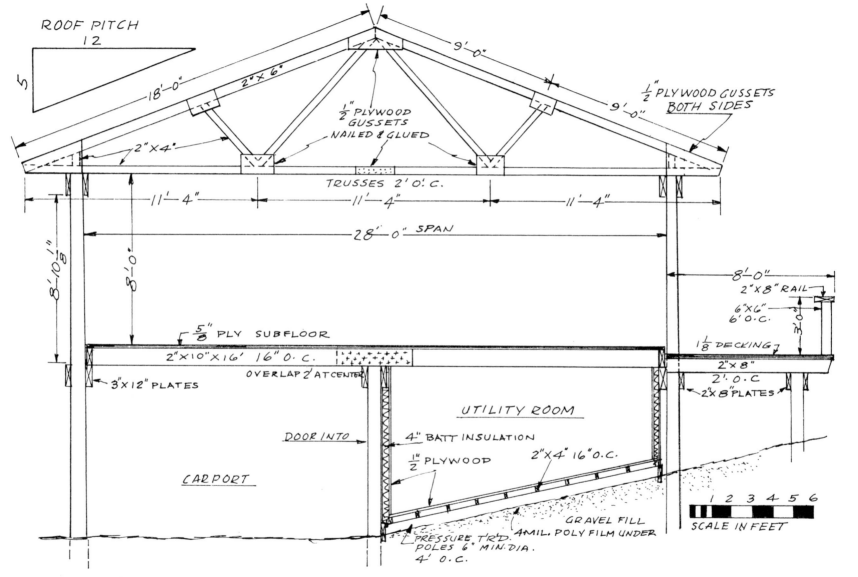

ROOF PITCH
12

5

18'-0"

2" X 6"

9'-0"

9'-0"

½" PLYWOOD GUSSETS
NAILED & GLUED

½" PLYWOOD GUSSETS
BOTH SIDES

2" X 4"

TRUSSES 2' O. C.

11'-4"

11'-4"

11'-4"

28'-0" SPAN

8'-10⅛"

8'-0"

8'-0"

2" X 8" RAIL

6" X 6"
6' O. C.

3'-0"

1⅛ DECKING

⅝" PLY SUBFLOOR

2" X 10" X 16' 16" O. C.

OVERLAP 2' AT CENTER

2" X 8"

2'. O. C

2" X 8" PLATES

3" X 12" PLATES

UTILITY ROOM

DOOR INTO

4" BATT INSULATION

½" PLYWOOD

2" X 4" 16" O.C.

CARPORT

GRAVEL FILL

PRESSURE TR'D.
POLES 6" MIN. DIA.
4' O. C.

4 MIL. POLY FILM UNDER

1 2 3 4 5 6

SCALE IN FEET

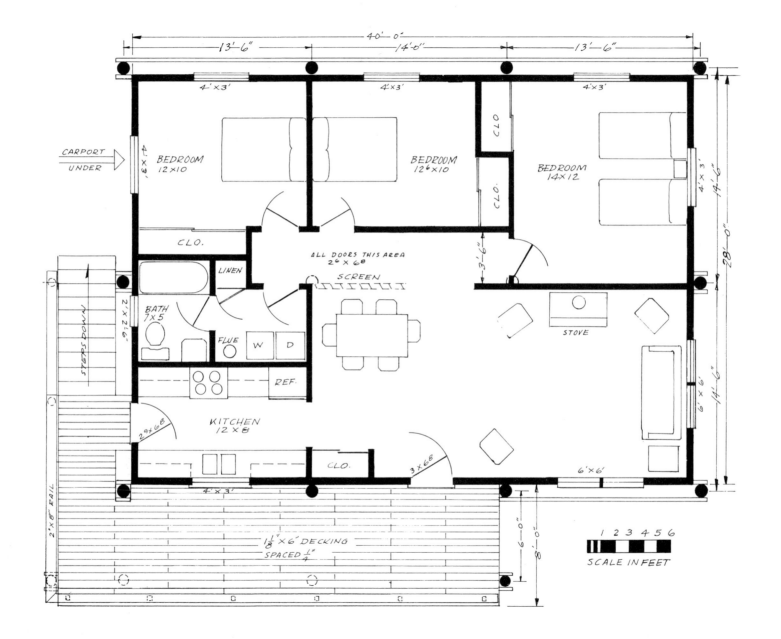

CARPORT
UNDER

BEDROOM
12×10

BEDROOM
12⁶×10

CLO

CLO

BEDROOM
14×12

4'×3'

4'×3'

4'×3'

4'×3'

40'-0"

13'-6"

14'-0"

13'-6"

14'-6"

28'-0"

CLO.

LINEN

ALL DOORS THIS AREA
2⁶ × 6⁸

SCREEN

3'-6"

2'×2'-6"

BATH
7×5

FLUE

W   D

STOVE

REF.

6'×6'

14'-6"

STEPS DOWN

2'×6'8

KITCHEN
12×8

CLO.

3×6⁸

6'×6'

4'×3'

6'-0"

8'-0"

2"×8" RAIL

1⅛"×6" DECKING
SPACED ¼"

1 2 3 4 5 6
SCALE IN FEET

INDEX

Am. Wood Preservers Inst. 7

Bracing, Permanent
    Gussets, Knees 21, 22

Bracing, Temporary 15

Buildings, Pole
    History 5, 6
    Permanence 7
    Uses 4

Carport (see Home Plans)

Conversion, Year 'Round 38

Cottage, Vacation (plans) 34-41

Drainage 9, 42

Floors, Framing 25, 26
    Insulation 25, 27
    Slab 25

Frost Line 14, 42

Girts 24, 42
    (also see Sidewall Constr.)

Heating 42

Holes, depth 11, 13
    digging 14
    location 11

Home, Year 'Round (plans) 42-47

Insulation, Floor 27
    Roof 28
    Wall 38

Joists, Floor 17, 26

Knee Braces 42
    (See Sidewall Constr.)

Load Chart (floors, roof) 28

Location, Site 11-13

Lumber, Standards 34

Necklace, Pole 20

Pads, Pole or Punch 14

Plates, Wall (locating, attaching) 9, 16, 17
    Inner Pole 19
    Ridge 18

Poles, Alignment 15, 34
    Embedment, Final 20
    Embedment, Permanent 15
    Preservatives 8, 9
    Setting 15
    Size 2, 14, 30
    Wood species 7

Preservatives 8, 9, 40

Purlins 23

Rafters 19

References 29

Roof, Insulation 28
    Sheathing 23

Roofing 23, 30

Shed, Storage (plans) 30-33

Sidewalls, Construction 23, 24
    Non load-bearing 34

Siding 25, 30

Soils 9

Splashboards 24

Strength, Poles (bending) 2
    Joists & Rafter span 28
    Snow Load & Wind 3, 17

Termites 25

Tools, needed 2, 4, 9, 14, 15

Trusses, Roof 42

Utility Room 25, 38

Water Supply 38, 42

Windows 30, 34

Wood, Rot Resistance 7, 40